FINANCIAL LITERACY

Steps To Building And Sustaining Wealth For Teens And Young Adults.

Timothy.A.Mangum

Copyright ©

All rights reserved. No part of this publication may be reproduced, distributed, or transmitted in any form or by any means, including photocopying, recording, or other electronic or mechanical methods, without the prior written permission of the publisher, except in the case of brief quotations embodied in critical reviews and certain other noncommercial uses permitted by copyright law.

Copyright © Timothy.A.Mangum,2022.

Table of content

Introduction

CHAPTER 1

CHAPTER 2

CHAPTER 3

CHAPTER 4

THE CONCLUSION

Introduction

Financial bondage is created by the mindset of using almost all of the money to pay off debt. A person must deal with stress, anxiety, and tension related to financial constraints. Without any room to work for himself, he needs to put in a lot of effort to meet his financial demand and duty. As a result, there is not enough money to cover basic demands. Such a mentality produces a certain way of thinking and living that makes reaching financial independence difficult. Lack of financial understanding and a long-term financial strategy might contribute to failure to reach financial independence. It results in a consumerist lifestyle where spending overtakes saving as the default option. A long-term financial plan includes moral life values like saving money before spending it, practical financial literacy, a budgeting strategy, a cash reserve of six months' worth of expenses, and sound investing strategies. These noble mental life ideals serve as a vision and a strong drive that create the foundation and power of limiting spending.

CHAPTER 1

Monetary Adaptability

When it comes to your financial stability, there are numerous ways to feel free. You want to be financially free, but the road you choose to get there will rely on your personality, way of life, culture, and short- and long-term objectives. Here are a few different perspectives on financial independence, obstacles you can face, and possible next actions. Financial independence is something many people aspire to. You want financial independence, but the route you choose to get there will likely rely on your personality, way of life, culture, and short- and long-term goals.

To assist you in defining what financial independence means to you, consider the following principles:

- getting a regular job and feeling in control of your finances
- maintaining momentum to meet your financial goals
- putting aside enough money in case anything goes wrong
- having sufficient funds to support a certain way of life

Your overall sense of financial security and confidence that you have enough money to meet your needs and goals without worry or stress is a result of all of these elements working together. But what is meant by financial independence is the capacity to manage your money and life in the way that is best for you.

There are a number of strategies to achieve financial independence, and each one has benefits and drawbacks. A financial plan and budget may be helpful for someone who wants to become financially independent because it offers them a clear picture of their current income and expenses and allows them to identify and choose the best methods to achieve their financial goals. A financial plan takes into account all aspects of a person's financial status.

In personal finance, a financial plan also known as an investment plan can concentrate on other particular topics, such as risk management, estate planning, and paying for education or retirement. earnings, asset worth, and withdrawal schedules. Financial planning is a thorough assessment of a person's present earnings and prospective financial situation utilizing known current factors to forecast the future.

Since they provide an estimate of income and expenditure for a certain future period of time, budgets are often developed and modified. A budget may be created by a person, a group of individuals, a business, a government, or pretty much anything else that makes and spends money.

As a consequence, you track your income and expenses with a budget either weekly or monthly, even though you often evaluate your progress with a financial plan on a quarterly or semi-annual basis. You may stay on the road to financial success by being aware of how your budget and financial plan interact. In general, you will make more progress on your financial plan the more strictly you stick to your budget.

Don't let money imprison you.

Financial hardships force us to act impulsively. This means being constrained by pricey lifestyles and investments that will deplete their funds for certain individuals.

If you want to get out of your cage or, better yet, completely avoid it, all you need is a plan you can employ to avoid falling for tactics that result in financial entrapment. There is a simple solution to avoid financial jail that is unaffected by your identification, albeit many people may find the execution difficult.

No matter what your salary is, what your job situation is, or whether you have a college degree or not, you have the same access to the tools that the affluent have been using for years to develop limitless wealth for themselves and their family.

<u>Become financially independent for the long term.</u>

Anyone may amass unending wealth and attain true financial freedom. The final definition of financial independence will vary somewhat depending on the individual. The common denominator is the capacity for self-control and the exercise of free will to act whichever one chooses.

In order to establish your financial independence, you must be able to show that you were able to sustain yourself on your own for a full year prior to the residence determination date.

How to Achieve Financial Freedom:

For a lot of people, having enough cash on hand, investments, and savings to sustain the kind of life they decide to live for themselves and their family is essential.
Too many people, unfortunately, lack financial freedom. The ongoing burden of increasing debt brought on by excessive spending keeps people from accomplishing their goals even in the absence of intermittent financial issues. When a significant event, such as a hurricane, an earthquake, or a pandemic, completely disrupts all plans, more safety net breaches become apparent.

Although almost everyone encounters difficulty, these 7 actions may help you avoid it.

1. Establish Your Life's Goals
What does financial freedom mean to you? It's a universal desire, yet it's a highly elusive goal. You must be exact when it comes to amounts and due dates. The clear your goals are, the more likely you are to achieve them.

Write out these three objectives:

- what is required for your way of life
- what your financial requirements are in order to make it happen, and
- When must a person start saving so much money?

As you go backward from your deadline age to your current age, set up financial checkpoints at regular intervals between the two dates. Make sure to carefully record all amounts and due dates on the target page, which you should place at the front of your financial binder.

2. Create a monthly spending plan.

The simplest way to guarantee that all expenses are paid and savings are proceeding as expected is to establish and stick to a monthly family budget. Additionally, sticking to your goals and renouncing the want to indulge are made easier when you have a timetable.

3. Continue Your Education in Finance

Review relevant changes in tax law to ensure that all adjustments and deductions are used to the fullest extent possible each year. Pay attention to market developments and financial news, and don't be hesitant to adjust your investment portfolio as required. Knowledge is the best defense against con artists that use novice investors to earn quick money.

4. Maintenance of Your Property

Everything that is well maintained, including property, lasts longer, from cars to shoes to clothes. Recognize the difference between the things you want and the ones you really need. Maintenance expenses are a smart investment since they are far cheaper than replacement expenses.

5. Keeping to your means

To achieve a frugal way of life, you need a mindset that emphasizes getting the most out of less, and it's easier than you would think. In fact, before becoming wealthy, many successful individuals developed the habit of living within their means.

Simple living is not difficult to adopt. It simply requires learning to distinguish between items you need and those you want and then making little adjustments that have a big impact on your financial well-being.

6. Utilize a financial adviser

Once you've amassed a substantial sum of money, either in liquid assets (cash or anything that can be turned into cash) or fixed assets, see a financial advisor help you stay on the right path (property or anything that cannot be converted into cash).

7. Keep Your Health.

Taking excellent care of your physical health also has a significant positive impact on your financial health. Your body needs regular upkeep as well.

Making an investment in your health is easy. It means following medical advice for any concerns you encounter, and seeing the dentist and doctor often. Numerous medical disorders may be helped by or even prevented by simple lifestyle changes like increased exercise and eating healthier.

On the other side, neglecting your health might have a negative short and long-term impact on your financial goals. When a company's allotted paid sick days are used up, there is a financial loss since some companies only permit a limited amount of sick days. Poor health may force early retirement and result in a lower monthly income for the remainder of your life. It may also raise insurance expenses and result in obesity and other food issues.

CHAPTER 2

Rapid Wealth Accumulation

Each person defines wealth differently. Some individuals define wealth as real estate ownership. Others define it as making profitable investments. Wealth, from a financial standpoint, is the total of your assets minus your liabilities.

The Best Method For Evaluating Your Wealth

- The market value of all of your assets, both tangible and intangible, should be subtracted from your obligations.
- Even though it could seem challenging, acquiring money is really rather simple. Actually, you don't even need a six-figure salary to realize your dreams. No of your age, if you're driven, you can amass wealth. Remember that doing so requires time.

Three Ways To Boost Your Wealth
The three ideas stated below may help you boost your finances.

1. You could make more money.

The most crucial stage in amassing money, whether you're just starting out or going through a transition, is having many streams of income. Here are a few tips for increasing your income and building up your savings rapidly.

- Enter the corporate world.

The wealthiest people in the world are business owners rather than employees. Entrepreneurship satisfies two needs for wealth creation: income and high returns on wealth obtained. So, if you have a business idea that can increase your revenue, put it into action. It's not necessary to run a large organization. You may start a small business and provide the services you are best at. For instance, the rise of the internet has made it possible for you to launch an entirely online business. If you're too busy to run the business yourself, you may hire someone to do it.

- work more jobs

Even if you have a job, you don't have to rely only on your income. You may run a side company effectively to increase your income. You might make money off your ability or hobby in your spare time.

Online side enterprises may be successfully run as long as you have an internet connection. These include:

acting as a virtual assistant.
independently written and edited.
Copywriting.
coach, consultant, and tutor online.
writing code, developing applications, etc.

Other part-time occupations without an internet connection include:

an adjunct professor at a local college

part-time instructor of gymnastics
Accounting, tax preparation, and independent teaching
starting to shop
driver for a side delivery or ride-sharing company

Improve Your Skills

There are two strategies to raise your income and investment returns. You may either increase your income or cut down on your expenditures. While focusing on the first, most people miss the second. You might increase your income by honing your skill set. This may include earning a degree or a special designation, all of which may result in a promotion and wage increase.

2. Spend More

Saving money is a critical step in building wealth. After you have enough cash on hand to pay your necessary costs, you should start saving. Remember that little sums saved often over time may result in significant wealth.

- Create a Budget

Projections of your spending and income should be part of your financial strategy. An essential tool for accumulating wealth is a budget. It gives you an overview of your expenditure and identifies areas where you may save costs.

To maintain a manageable budget, it is advised to create a new one each month. Can you imagine a sailor without a compass? When someone spends their money recklessly, it seems like that. A severe financial collapse will probably be experienced by such a person in the future.

One of the most well-liked and effective budgeting techniques is the 50/30/20 rule. This method suggests that you should set aside 50% of your income for basics like housing, food, and healthcare. A 30% budgetary allotment is utilized for luxuries and extras like shopping. The remaining 20% should be allocated to savings since it is the most important allocation.

- Establish an emergency fund.

Emergency preparedness kits make it easier for you to prepare for unanticipated events like losing your job. Such occurrences might derail your attempts to accumulate money if you don't have emergency savings. The investment might be sold or debt can be accumulated.

Your finances begin to decline when you are in debt. In addition, you'll have to pay interest on the loan. If you sell your investment, you forfeit the money and earnings you would have otherwise received. To avoid such occurrences, set up an emergency fund as a safety net to pay for unanticipated bills.

3. Invest

When you've decided how much money you want to save each month, it's time to start investing. When you invest your money, you make more money. You could become extremely wealthy by investing your income in the stock market and real estate over time.

- Stock market

Buying stock in a company is among the simplest and quickest ways to make more money. By acquiring shares, you may join the company's shareholders and take control of the business. Stocks, which provide the largest return on investment but carry a disproportionately higher level of risk than other assets, are made simple and risk-free to invest in via exchange-traded funds. With a well-informed diversification strategy, you can reduce risks and boost earnings.

- True Estate

By investing in real estate investment trusts, you may gain from the real estate market without having any direct involvement. REITs are essentially the stock of firms that buy and sell real estate. Mortgage companies are included in this category.

But earning money is not a tough process; if you put in the effort and are disciplined, you can rapidly expand your fortune. Before starting this adventure, it's important to educate oneself about money. After doing that, you should have no trouble completing the following stages and eventually accumulating wealth.

Many people overlook retirement accounts when it comes to saving money. You'll accumulate wealth over time in addition to retirement savings.

Seven principles for strategic wealth management.

1. Take charge and move swiftly.

2. Align your family's and your business's interests around wealth-building goals and strategies.

3. Create a culture of accountability.

4. Delegate, respect the independence, and assign power.

5. While diversifying, maintain your focus.

6. Always err on the side of simplicity.

7. Develop future family leaders' capacity for managing finances.

CHAPTER 3

Establishing Your Wealth

There is a wealth of financial information available to us nowadays. There are views here and there. Each activity may be approached in around 15 distinct ways. But it's essential to remember that when it comes to building and preserving your wealth, simplicity is preferred.

The only things you need to do are a few simple disciplines that you practice every day to reach your financial potential. You get your desired life in this way. For both your and my purposes, I would change this.

These simple disciplines really are just that basic. They are easy to understand. No specialist knowledge is needed. Maybe this is the case because common sense is at the core of the best simple disciplines.

They are the behaviors you know are healthy for you and that you should engage in. However, they require the most difficult to complete. If it were easy, everyone would be successful. Finding success is simple, but it's not necessarily easy, and I think that's a key distinction. You have to be willing to do things that other people avoid.

A FEW POINTERS FOR MAINTAINING AND ESTABLISHING YOUR WEALTH

Understanding your financial potential is simple, not challenging. But if you adhere to the clear instructions we've covered here, I'm certain it will become easier.

I can say that since I have firsthand knowledge of it. In my clients' daily routines and financial philosophies, I played a significant part in creating these simple guidelines, and I have constantly seen their effectiveness. You can do it too, but you must first change a behavior that has become automatic.

You can build and retain your wealth by following these fundamental principles.

1. What drives you to work for a living?

Why do you invest in any of it or work for it? What can you do if you have money? How is your current financial condition advancing and supporting your basic values? Since successful people are aware of the answers to these questions, you should as well. If not, nothing is worth fighting for. You cannot effectively manage your money without this.

2. Examine your innermost aspirations.

One problem with traditional financial planning is that it is based on a needs analysis and a scarcity mindset. It limits the amount of money you can make before you even start your quest. However, taking into account what you really want out of life encourages you to develop an attitude of plenty. The wall between what is and what may be is torn down in this manner.

3. Live within your means;

if your lifestyle is always at its highest level, you will never succeed financially. I vowed. By choosing to live reasonably rather than extravagantly, you may avoid maintaining a deceptively humble lifestyle. Naturally, because you are striving for the life you desire, it is OK to indulge. However, that doesn't mean you should give up on your efforts altogether.

4. Pay yourself first.

If you are unable to develop the comparatively easy discipline of saving, everything else in your financial life will need to work harder to make up the slack. Keep 3-6 months' worth of liquid expenses on hand while aiming to save 15% to 20% of your income annually. It's also a good idea to have six to twelve months' worth of near-liquid cash on hand.

AUTOMATIC DEDUCTIONS - Using automatic deductions is one of the simplest ways to consistently make sure that you pay yourself last.

5. The capacity to invest and save for the future will be severely hampered if you have a lot of high-interest debt. And at this point, unless investing brings in the 15% or more interest or more that you are probably paying on that debt, it is pointless for you to invest.

6. Describe your investment philosophies.

This document outlines your investment strategies as well as your core values and objectives. With the help of this document, which serves as a reminder of the reasoning behind your chosen investment strategy, you can protect yourself from market fluctuations. It serves as a reminder of your financial "why." You shouldn't invest in anything that doesn't meet this requirement.

7. Protection first.

Think about everything you've created. Think about everything you will build in the future. Think about what would transpire if everything failed now. Is this not ugly? Because of this, success doesn't depend on your financial situation. It depends on how well you protect your life's work from potential dangers. If you don't do this, nothing you're attempting to accomplish will matter.

8. Assemble your mighty squad.

You must assemble a group of your most dependable advisors to help you lead yourself toward financial freedom. They should all be familiar with one another and meet often on your behalf. It is wise to discuss potential effects on your whole financial condition before making adjustments to one area of your financial life. In an ideal world, you would have one financial advisor who would also act as your personal assistant to handle all of your financial affairs.

9. Recognize the distinctions between risk and volatility.

Risk is only the possibility that your investment will result in a loss of money. The likelihood grows as the threat level rises. Simply put, your returns are unaffected. The level of variation that a portfolio may experience is called volatility. The higher the volatility, the more erratic your compound returns might be. Volatility affects your returns directly and also reduces your wealth. So your top priority should be lowering volatility.

10. Time spent in the market is what counts.

Your wealth could be harmed by poor stock selection, poor market timing, excessive confidence, and other factors. You won't typically select the winning stock or enter or exit at the ideal time.

11. Little changes might have a big effect.

You don't always need to make substantial changes to reach your financial potential. Consider investing 10% of your $100,000 monthly salary in a portfolio that yields a 7% return. Your earnings after 35 years will be $1,479,134. But what if your savings rate only increased by 1%? In the end, you would have $1,627,048. Savings of only one more pitiful percent would reach $146,914.

12. Think of yourself as wealthy when it comes to estate planning.

Rich people have three main aims when it comes to the planning of estate:
1) Continue to generate sufficient income,
2) Keep my assets safe from creditors,

3) Permanently evade the wealth transfer tax. Trusts are a fantastic tool for doing this. And no, estate planning and trusts are not exclusively for the very affluent. Everyone needs to have a fundamental estate strategy that, at the absolute least, consists of a will and durable power of attorney.

CHAPTER 4

BUILDING GENERATIONAL WEALTH

On the list of the richest people in the world, there are a few self-made barons, but the vast majority of aristocrats have never known anything else because they were born into wealth. It's known as generational wealth, and it's not just for the top 1%.

By accumulating money, even little wealth, expanding it, safeguarding and defending it, and passing it down to benefit those who will come after them, average people who make sensible decisions may provide their children and grandchildren an edge.

Of course, it's easier said than done, but common people from common backgrounds can increase their homes' equity, start businesses, make wise investments, and perhaps most importantly, learn, plan, and get professional assistance to

make sure that what they build isn't wasted by this generation or the one after.
The Definitive Guide to Growing, Protecting, Enjoying, and Passing on Your Wealth. It requires open communication with family members, addressing topics that are personal in nature.

Employ a professional and keep an eye on your taxes.

One thing almost all people who successfully pass wealth to future generations have in common is that they don't do it alone.

"It's hard to forecast what the forthcoming trends will be," said Smallwood, "but estate taxes have a history of eroding wealth. You could have amassed a significant sum of personal money before inheriting extra cash. In such a case, your tax bracket can increase. Lack of preparation might cause wealth losses of between 40% and 50% over multiple generations. Financial experts may help you in setting up layers of asset protection, such as revocable trusts, life insurance, spousal lifetime access trusts, and wills, to secure inherited money for both you and future generations.

Consider a career in construction.

One of the most trustworthy methods to transfer money from one generation to the next is to buy businesses with real estate tied to them. They are given an asset that generates cash flow from the moment they take control of it, allowing them to avoid the initial period of company growth. Apartment building owners get to enjoy the building's income flow, grow equity via compelled asset appreciation, and gain from the tax benefits of sizable real estate.

Invest

Investment in real estate may be thrilling but also somewhat unpredictable. Less interesting but more dependable investments are likely to perform better over the long run.

The best sector in the world to invest in is property and casualty insurance. You might become extremely wealthy by focusing on insurance.

Make several different revenue streams.

The recent pandemic showed that those with many income streams are more likely to overcome unanticipated problems than people with large amounts of money. Achieving that level of financial security will benefit future generations.

Young people should work to diversify their income streams so they aren't dependent on one, and they can turn their interests into side businesses that can boost their income. If their side business succeeds, they might think about quitting their job and starting their own business full-time, giving them greater control over their financial development.

THE CONCLUSION

Concerning the aforementioned justifications, it is possible to conclude that a rise in income is insufficient to obtain financial independence. The practical conceptual financial concepts must form the basis of applied philosophy that manifests in a certain way of thinking, way of living, and way of doing actions that lead to financial independence. In terms of personal conviction, self-denial, choices, and decision-making, applied philosophical conceptual concepts in finance are embodied in the real world as human concrete action. The intersection of human activity and personal belief in God is therefore formed through choice, action direction, and decision. Therefore, human concrete action can serve as an icon of faith in which a person emerges from himself and expresses response, expectation, hope, trust, and spiritual aspiration to achieve financial freedom. Human concrete action is the culmination of human-rooted conceptual principles, thought, and personal belief. There is a strong belief and motivation that are expressed in the single deed, serving as a symbol of faith in the real world. Faith as an attitude contains a personal conviction and a surrendering attitude to God, which are supportive to enliven faith and financial freedom achievement in the recent practical financial life, as opposed to faith as a content, which is God, divine instructions, and revelation in the Holy Scriptures.

www.ingramcontent.com/pod-product-compliance
Lightning Source LLC
Chambersburg PA
CBHW050320220526
45465CB00005B/2066